Narcissism

Deal With Mother-Child Relationships And Learn How To Recover From Emotional And Narcissistic Abuse

(The Guide To Codependency Recovery)

Markus Keller

TABLE OF CONTENT

What Is Narcissism?... 1

Diagnoses 12

What Makes Narcissism A Problem? 21

Various Forms Of Narcissists..27

Techniques For Gaslighting And Humiliation..........36

Choosing The Right Words To Use 54

The Serious And Long-Lasting Consequences Of Living In A Narcissistic Society 59

Disorder Of The Narcissistic Personality 80

What Is Narcissistic Abuse...95

Understanding Anxiety And Depression Disorders Of The Mind 116

How To Avoid And Manage A Narcissist................. 123

Potential Roots Of Narcissism 147

Relationship With A Narcissist..................................... 152

What Is Narcissism?

The Greek story of a hunter called Narcissus is where the word "narcissism" originated. He was the hunky, haughty child of a deity and a nymph. He didn't leave the water till he passed away because he was so drawn to his own reflection there.

The word "narcissism" is now used to describe anybody who is motivated by their own vanity and seeks to please themselves. It may also be described as a profound admiration and interest in oneself, especially in terms of one's physical and intellectual traits. In a nutshell, pride and haughtiness lead to narcissism.

Mirrors are particularly beloved by narcissists because they are always interested in and self-conscious about their looks. Although the narcissist lacks the humility of a well-balanced person, they also give off the impression of having a high amount of self assurance.

When someone threatens their self-esteem, narcissists have a propensity to become very protective, and some even become angry towards the person who is posing the danger. While some narcissists try to hide their insecurities with their inflated egos, others truly feel quite happy with themselves and lead an outwardly genteel existence.

Due to its impact on the individual and society, narcissism is a topic of research in the social sciences. There is recognition of a good kind of narcissism, which should not be confused with egocentrism (which is more accurately described as being self-centered or selfish).

When you first encounter a narcissist, he or she often exudes charm and physical attractiveness. But the more you get to know a narcissist, the more you see how hard it is for them to keep up strong, lifelong bonds. Once a person turns 30, narcissistic behavior often starts to decline.

The disorder known as narcissistic personality

Once narcissism interferes with a person's life and the lives of others around them, it is considered a disease. Narcissistic Personality Disorder is what this is known as, and it is more severe and uncommon than narcissism. People who with this disorder believe they are the center of the universe. They therefore lack empathy, regard themselves as the only thing that matters, and are continually looking for praise from others. A person with this illness is quite likely to be someone who others see as being very self-assured, egotistical, manipulative, and needy.

Narcissists feel they are entitled to preferential treatment above everyone else and emphasize achieving extreme personal objectives, such as fame. They often overestimate their talents and take rash, impulsive actions because they think they will always succeed.

To achieve her aims, a narcissist won't think twice about stepping on others' toes, and she often exaggerates her success, significance, and achievements. A narcissist often fantasizes about achieving impossible levels of success, strength, beauty, and intelligence. He has a short fuse and becomes very envious if someone pays attention to someone else. When it reaches its peak, the Narcissistic Personality Disorder renders a person emotionally insensitive to others.

Narcissists refuse to seek medical attention for their disorder, hence there is sadly no cure for narcissistic personality disorder. Include narcissists in social groups and community events as a means of encouraging them to become more involved and real with others.

Potential Roots of Narcissism

What triggers narcissism is a topic of continuous discussion. It could result from a combination of genetics and environment. The result of innate physical and intellectual characteristics may be narcissism. A person who is physically attractive often believes themselves to be better than others, particularly if others around them support this notion. Environmental factors, such as admiration for a famous person who shows narcissistic characteristics, may also cause narcissism.

Narcissists may develop as a result of how their parents treated them, according to Sigmund Freud. Narcissists are often those who either had too much or too little affection from their parents; narcissism is much more prone to develop if a kid receives a mix of both sorts of treatment. Future psychologists tend to agree with this hypothesis and add that because of the discrepancy, people experience internal insecurity and respond by trying to win others' admiration. Because they are first drawn to the narcissist's charm but later reject him after getting to know him better, peers also contribute to this inconsistent behavior and the growth of narcissism.

The reality is that there are a ton of additional elements that might affect how a narcissist thinks. These will be covered in greater detail in the next chapters.

HOW TO CONTROL A NEGLECTIST

If you're dating someone with NPD, you've undoubtedly already been through a lot.

It may be quite tiring to be in a relationship with someone who constantly criticizes, denigrates, gaslights, and refuses to commit to you.

the best way to prepare for a split.

Always keep in mind that you deserve better.

Strengthen your connections with your empathetic friends.

Build a network of loved ones and friends who will support you and act as a reminder of what is sincere.

Insist that your companion see a therapist right away.

Self-help is suggested.

A person with NPD cannot be changed or made happy by showing them enough love or by caving in to their wants and demands. Since they will never be tuned into you, sympathetic to your experiences, or in sync with you, says Grace, you will always feel empty after dealing with them.

She goes on to say that narcissists are unable to feel satisfied in relationships or in any other area of their lives since nothing in their lives is ever special enough for them.

In essence, since they will never be content with themselves, you will never be enough for them.

The best line of action is to cut off communication. Give no explanation to them. Don't give someone a second chance. Grace continues, "Disconnect from them and don't give them another chance."

Because someone with NPD will likely attempt to contact you and harass you with calls or messages after they have fully digested the rejection, Krol suggests blocking them to help you stick to your choice.

Remember that your partner is not being diagnosed by this book.

Instead, this essay's goal is to outline unacceptable behavior within the context of a loving, fair relationship. Not all of your partner's behaviors may be classified as narcissistic. Instead, it's a great opportunity to reexamine how well your partnership is doing.

Diagnoses

Professionals are competent to identify narcissistic personality disorder. The specialist will evaluate you or a loved one's condition using the aforementioned symptoms as a starting point, but they will also ask you some more detailed questions. Since general practitioners and family doctors are often not qualified or prepared to detect personality disorders, only a trained specialist should make the diagnosis. If they think you could have a personality issue, they will nonetheless recommend you to the appropriate person.

Sadly, there is no laboratory, blood, or genetic testing available to identify this condition. Additionally, since they do not think they are unwell, persons who experience this disease often avoid getting care. When this problem first starts to affect a person's personal or professional life, they won't seek medical attention. This often occurs when people are too stressed to cope with life's events and their coping mechanisms are no longer effective.

Therefore, only mental health care specialists are qualified to diagnose this disease. They do so by comparing a patient's life history to their symptoms. The choice as to whether or not you are a narcissist will be made by them.

Tests

The test is really easy to complete, and the exam is rather straightforward. Since narcissism does not manifest physically, a doctor will only collect samples or draw blood if they suspect that you may be unwell. Otherwise, a psychological assessment, signs, and symptoms will be used to make the diagnosis.

Narcissism's characteristics may resemble other symptoms of many personality disorders rather closely, and it's not uncommon to have several personality disorders at once.

Getting Ready for the Meeting

If you do not already have a psychologist that you regularly see, you should start by going to your primary care physician. If you require a diagnosis or to have your mental health examined, they will point you in the direction of the appropriate person.

Steps to Take

You should compile a list of the following items before your appointment:

Symptoms you may have had or are now experiencing, as well as how long they have been present. List your symptoms and the reasons you are experiencing them, if you are aware of them. What, for instance, causes you to feel angry or hopeless?

Information about you that may be connected to your disease, such as terrible incidents from the past or a present source of great stress.

Your mental and physical health history, together with any diseases for which you have received a diagnosis, are all included in your medical information.

the dosages of any vitamins, supplements, and prescription drugs you may be taking. Contrary to popular belief, drugs—whether prescribed or over-the-counter—may have negative effects on the mind that might mimic narcissism.

a list of inquiries you could make to your mental health professional to kick-start your recovery.

You should bring a trusted family member with you to your appointment so that you can feel safe. Additionally, you should invite them so that they can recall the specifics. You could also want to make sure it's someone who has known you for a long time and will be able to provide the psychologist with useful information or ask questions that may be beneficial.

Questions to Ask Initially

To ensure that nothing is forgotten during your visit, you may wish to bring a list similar to this—or perhaps this list—to your doctor.

Narcissistic personality disorder: what is it?

Is it possible that I suffer from another personality or mental disorder?

What is the objective of my care?

Which medical procedures do you believe would be most beneficial for me?

Do you anticipate that the therapy will enhance my quality of life, and if so, by how much?

How often and for how long do I need to visit a therapist?

Would family therapy or group therapy be more beneficial in my situation?

Do you have any drugs that I may use to help?

I have (insert ailment here) and would want to know how to effectively handle both my narcissism and this or these problems.

Do you have any publications or websites you may suggest I look at?

What is the first step I need to take to start a safe, effective treatment plan?

The Consultation

A mental health professional will interrogate you extensively. They are trying to determine if you have the illness and what your symptoms are. They could inquire about some of the things below to better understand what you are going through. As you respond, be kind to them and remember that they are attempting to assist you.

You'll be questioned about your symptoms.

How long have the symptoms been present and when did they start?

What is the duration of the symptoms?

How do they impact your social, professional, academic, and personal lives?

How do you respond when someone rejects or criticizes you? What do you think?

Do you maintain tight, intimate ties? Can you provide a justification if you don't?

What are the achievements that have changed your life?

What are your future objectives?

How do you react when someone requests your assistance?

When someone displays grief, fear, or other challenging emotions toward you, how do you feel and respond?

What memories of your youth do you have? How well did you get along with your guardians? What would you say about your early years?

Has anybody else in your family ever had a mental health issue diagnosed? Who?

Have you received treatment for another mental illness? If so, which therapies gave you the greatest results?

How often do you use alcohol or illicit substances?

Are you currently receiving care for any further medical conditions?

You may proceed to the therapy step when your doctor diagnoses you with the condition or another disorder.

What Makes Narcissism A Problem?

If you consider the typical person's life goals, there are certainly a lot on the list. Many individuals look for jobs, houses, families, relationships, and hobbies. This view is distorted in the mind of someone with narcissistic personality disorder. The person could want all of the aforementioned things, but only if they are not given top priority. On the outside, it may seem like effort and attention are being spent on achieving life objectives, but needing approval is really one of the most prominent features experienced by someone with NPD. However, the concentration is often deceptive -- All of these actions are taken by narcissists in an effort to win acclaim.

Although the inflated ego may not seem to be a threat right now, it can eventually cause many relationships to fall apart.

Aggression may result from narcissism; if the recognition isn't good enough, this is when the negative impacts happen. A narcissist may transform swiftly from content to intolerant. These folks have no compassion for other people. This is why it may be simple for a narcissist to become close to someone before easily letting them go. It is a risky social contact that might emotionally harm the narcissist as well as the other party.

Someone who engages in excessive narcissistic conduct is unlikely to really care about your emotions or your quality of life. The majority of the time, narcissists do not have empathy. A narcissist will likely think it is not their issue if you are suffering. There won't be any effort made to console or encourage you. This is why spending extended periods of time with someone who has NPD may be tiring. Any intimate connection with someone that is not reciprocated might have negative, protracted effects. When you are close to a narcissist, it might seem as if you are being underappreciated by others around you, as we have all experienced on occasion.

Anybody may develop narcissism.

Although everyone may act in a narcissistic manner, males are more likely than any other gender to have narcissistic personality disorder. It is crucial to realize that, regardless of the mental disorder, including NPD, you cannot self-diagnose. This is a complicated condition that is unique to each individual. Even though no two cases will appear precisely same, the symptoms will always be present. Getting a professional opinion is the quickest and most effective approach to evaluate if a degree of narcissism is problematic. Just be aware that the condition is not exclusive. People of all ages are diagnosed with NPD, even though it often results from childhood trauma.

It is a condition that has a strong connection to one's own happiness; individuals who suffer may come off as tough on the outside but are really suffering greatly on the inside. This emotional disguising results in a hard exterior that is supposed to conceal weakness. Regardless of how much success they may have, a person with NPD could not feel that life is interesting or rewarding enough. All of these emotions are legitimate and common for people to experience, but how they are handled determines whether or not coping techniques are healthy.

As soon as helpful advise is given, narcissists will falter. For instance, "Johnny, I think it might work better to use watercolor paint instead of acrylic paint for blending."

For someone with NPD, hearing this phrase may come off as criticism, sending them into a tailspin of insecurity. Although it wasn't intended to insult or denigrate anybody, a narcissist can find it to be triggering. Oftentimes, aggressive or cruel conduct may ensue. He or she could interpret the counsel as an admission of incompetence rather than taking it seriously. This is a risky tipping point for strong emotions, as you could expect. These behaviors will persist until you decide it is time to stop them since the narcissistic person is not going to be sensitive to your emotions.

Being close to someone who has NPD may be quite perplexing. It often makes you wonder whether you're being too sensitive: Am I responding too strongly?

When it comes to making you feel horrible about yourself, a narcissist has no compassion. Keep in mind that you won't be the first priority. This is a harsh truth that might be difficult to embrace. This is particularly true for those who date narcissists.

Various Forms Of Narcissists

Know your narcissistic personality types? Apart from researchers, doctors, psychologists, and psychotherapists, very few people really are familiar with all of the many sorts. For the average person, a narcissist is just who they are—a narcissist. When working with one, types actually don't matter.

However, how a narcissist expresses themselves and should be dealt with depends on the kind.

We have now read about their sense of entitlement and their sense that they are deserving of special treatment. They live in a dream world where they believe they are the most accomplished and dominant person. Additionally, we now understand that they lie to cover up their anxieties and that they have very fragile egos that they guard at all costs. The description of a person with NPD is completed by their lack of empathy, their tendency to exploit others, and their manipulation of others to further their own ends.

But there are many levels of narcissism. Not all NPD sufferers fit into the same categories. There are three main categories of narcissists, each with a unique combination of characteristics. One kind may have the same goal while others preserve their fragile egos in various methods.

It's interesting that there are sub-categories that represent how the attributes may be shown to others within the three kinds that the researchers determined.

Professionals in the field of mental health and researchers sometimes disagree. The same kind is known by a variety of labels that are often used. Even when the same type or sub-type is being defined, labels might be applied to two categories that are unrelated.

With so many different kinds and sub-types of narcissists, it may be challenging to identify the type being discussed and comprehend them (Milstead, Ph.D., Kristen, 2018).

Five Sub-Types and Three Types

According to studies, there are three main categories of narcissists and five subgroups. Various scholars use distinct language to categorically identify them. They describe the relationships between them in detail.

Three Major Narcissistic Types

Traditional narcissist

Narcissists who are grandiose, exhibitionistic, or very functional - When people hear the word "narcissist," they often think of these individuals as "typical narcissists."

These people are narcissists who need attention, anticipate flattery and praise from others, boast about their accomplishments, and have an attitude of entitlement that makes them believe they deserve special treatment. The most overt kind of narcissism is this one.

They consider themselves to be the most significant and influential person in the world. By bragging about their achievements, they want to inspire envy or admiration in others or both.

This particular narcissist may be charismatic and endearing. You can be drawn into their admiring area if their goal matches the achievements they brag about.

They get disinterested if the talk shifts its attention from them to someone else. They dislike having to share the limelight with others. They seldom like sharing the spotlight with anybody else since they believe they are the most important topic.

Ironically, despite their desperate need to be acknowledged and feel significant, they always think they are better than everyone they interact with.

Negative narcissists

Toxic narcissists are the kind of narcissists who are very manipulative and exploitative, and whose features are generally regarded to be comparable to psychopathic and sociopathic tendencies in addition to being antisocial. This sort of narcissist differs from the descriptions of the other two primary categories, classical and susceptible, in that they typically have a sadistic streak.

Their first priority is dominance and control, and they will steal, cheat, lie, and use aggressiveness to get it while showing no guilt whatsoever. They could take pleasure in other people's pain.

Narcissists at Risk

Compensatory, fragile, or covert narcissists Despite feeling superior to everyone they encounter, they do not like being in the limelight. In fact, they detest it. In contrast to receiving special treatment for themselves, they often want to be connected with those who they perceive to be unique. By showing great generosity to others or attempting to win their compassion, people may get the attention and respect they need to feel more valuable (Milstead, Ph.D., Kristen, 2018).

Narcissists who are weak emotionally may deplete others. This is due to their emotional sensitivity as well as how demanding they may be. They want to be recognized as the ideal beings that they are by others.

Because their imagined life doesn't reflect the reality they really live, this kind of narcissist is more likely to experience depression.

Recognize that there are myths about personality disorders and mental disease. Some individuals intentionally harm themselves or threaten to do so to get attention. In light of this, realize that vulnerable narcissists make threats to kill themselves in order to get attention. They seldom ever follow through on their threats, however.

Techniques For Gaslighting And Humiliation

What is gaslighting, and where does the phrase originate from? A movie named Gaslight is where the phrase "gaslighting" first appeared. The spouse in the movie repeatedly adjusts the antique gaslight. And he denies that anybody is turning the light on and off when his wife questions him about it. The woman gradually starts to question her own reality. She then becomes detached from reality. Finally, she loses her mind. Denial of someone's reality, whether intentional or not, is gaslighting.

A kind of emotional abuse is gaslighting. When person A casts doubt on person B's actuality, person B is left feeling quite perplexed. The narcissist uses this technique as kind of a hallmark tactic, and they act in this way to shield their ego. The narcissist doesn't care how much their gaslighting and denial techniques injure someone else in the process.

An instrument of emotional abuse and manipulation, gaslighting. The partner on the receiving end finds it annoying when you question someone else's reality. They believe they are maybe going insane and losing their sense of reality. There are several covert indicators that someone is trying to gaslight you. When someone informs you of the following, pay close attention:

-It's not proper for you to feel that way.

I'm sorry you decided to make yourself feel that way, but it seems like you're exaggerating

Why can't you let go of the past? -You are too sensitive.

You are being too dramatic, no one will love you as much as I do, and that never occurred. You shouldn't feel that way; I believe you to be mentally sick; you need assistance; and why can't you get a job.

Stop acting like a victim. Why are you so furious all the time?

These statements undermine your feelings and experiences when they are made to you. It is dehumanizing when people make remarks like that, as if they have no right to feel what they do. It takes away a person's humanity and natural capacity for feeling. It is comparable to telling someone they are hungry when they obviously are not. Imagine telling someone they are fatigued when they really feel refreshed.

The best course of action when faced with these statements is to leave the discussion since there is no chance of victory. The narcissist will continue to gaslight you and show no sign of understanding your emotions, no matter how robotically you express them. They'll keep twisting and manipulating your remarks to further abuse you. Avoid fighting overall since it will not resolve anything.

Deflection is another sign that your spouse or another person is gaslighting you. Gaslighting takes the shape of a deflection, which takes place when you want to sit down and discuss something important for the relationship's advancement. Your narcissists shift the conversation away from your issues as soon as you start to voice them. Despite the fact that you are being reasonable and discussing a current issue, they try to divert your attention by bringing up an irrelevant or old problem. The problem with deflections is that they create a circumstance in which you appear awful and are at fault.

The discussion is done if you find yourself in a scenario where you have to constantly bring someone back to the present circumstance. Due to their avoidance behaviors, you may have to accept that you won't have the dialogue. When someone utterly rejects your reality, it is the third kind of gaslighting. They'll remark something along the lines of: That never occurred.

When we are informed that something never occurred, we often question our actions and go back over what transpired. The narcissist will react angrily or deflect when we obtain proof that something really did happen and tell them the truth. Narcissists dislike being exposed for the flaws in their gaslighting. When you feel the need to record your interactions or write a letter or email, it is a solid sign that you are being gaslighted.

You could believe that if you express all of your feelings and worries in writing, the narcissist will read them since there are no interruptions, but this is untrue. Narcissists don't pay attention. Because of this, you spend your days and weekends writing or considering the best way to express yourself, but as soon as you do, their answers just grow worse. They'll turn everything against you.

The easiest course of action in situations like these is to quit the discussion since you are not progressing. Any human being should not consistently engage in any of these undesirable behaviors. It is really draining to always have to defend and prove oneself. Your mental well-being and sanity are negatively impacted by this whole process, which resembles a deranged mind game. To deal with and recover from the release of emotional abuse, you do need resources and expert assistance.

You can assume that the narcissist is aware of what they are doing. And the answer is difficult since some people may be aware of it while others are unaware of their habits and behaviors. The narcissist's fundamental insecurity drives them to be solely determined to preserve their reality and view of the world. They are actively considering influencing you when they are in defense mode. Instead, they lack empathy, which prevents them from considering how their actions impact the people they care about. The narcissist believes they are entitled to do it, thus they believe they have the right to. They also don't want to be found out and discovered since they are vulnerable.

This explains why narcissists act defensively and seek to cover up any mistakes or failures they may have made. They use gaslighting as a way to escape difficult circumstances. Because they do not want to cope with your emotions and experiences, they minimize them. Because they do it unconsciously, minimising is a sort of gaslighting that is more damaging because it is a passive process.

The victim of gaslighting has an overwhelming sense of self-doubt as a result of the process of ignoring and downplaying their emotions or realities over time. This connection is poisonous and detrimental to your emotional and mental well-being. It is clear that your relationship is unhealthy if you are at a stage where you are questioning if you are doing anything wrong for bringing up a subject.

You are simultaneously becoming invisible and losing your sense of self as you live in constant dread of not being able to express your demands or your emotions. You ignore the fact that your self-worth is eroding and put others before yourself. The promises of improvement and the occasions when it seems as if your spouse is making progress are what maintain you in the long run. With a positive outlook, you continue to play the long game, believing that you can either help them change or repair them. But nothing will improve until the narcissist asks for assistance.

How might being the victim of gaslighting lessen some of the suffering and angst? Avoid participating, exit the discussion, end it, and acknowledge that certain issues and circumstances won't be resolved. Accept your connection with your narcissistic spouse as it is and their genuine state. Seek assistance and rely on your support network; they are your lifeline.

Do You Have a Narcissist on Your Hands?

You must recognize the following traits in a person in order to determine if you are living with a narcissist or are mostly dealing with narcissism:

Pride and a feeling of superiority. A narcissist cannot comprehend how someone else may be smarter, more knowledgeable, more attractive, more skilled, or more intelligent than them. Narcissists believe they are the most capable people and that they always come out on top.

They want total control over everyone and everything. They quickly get angry when things don't go their way since they think they are always correct. They take it personally if you disagree with them on anything.

They tend to despise persons of low rank and want to interact solely with high profile individuals. They aren't afraid to use their influence to further their personal agendas. They constantly seek for the attention, affirmation, and validation of others in order to maintain a healthy sense of self. They always seek perfection in circumstances and people, which is an unreasonable goal. They make sure to bug you to shower them with more praise if they believe you aren't showing them enough attention or making them feel appreciated. They have the opportunity to become even more irate and unsatisfied as a result. Additionally, they believe that they have the right to criticize how others act or what they decide to do. They often feel jealous of others but believe that others feel jealous of them. They fail to accept responsibility for their conduct. As a result, they strive to be moral instructors to everyone they see behaving contrary to their ideals. They like blaming you or someone else when anything goes wrong or when you attempt to confront them about something.

You should investigate the causes of narcissistic behavior now that you are aware of how to spot it in a person. Despite the fact that the reasons of narcissistic behavior are largely unknown, elements like unbalanced parenting, genetics, or neuroscience are likely to be to blame.

Additionally, you should be aware that some individuals are born narcissists. Even if someone is a narcissist due of the setting and milieu in which they were reared, some of it is still ingrained in them. While we'll examine some potential origins of narcissism, this doesn't mean that we should ignore any narcissistic abuse that has occurred. It is important to understand how narcissism develops in order to discover a cure and a way out.

Narcissism and parenting style

Evidently, a person's off-kilter upbringing gives narcissism an opportunity to develop relatively early in life. A youngster is more prone to become narcissistic over time if their parents give them excessive praise or continual criticism. Most often, individuals who get excessive amounts of love and admiration grow up to be grandiose narcissists, whereas those who don't get the support and care they need grow up to be weak narcissists.

People often develop narcissism as a psychological defense against severe abuse, criticism, or neglect during their early years. Due to the humiliation, anxiety, uncertainty, or deprivation they experienced as children, they feel emotionally wounded. So, despite their arrogant demeanors, they are lonely, isolated, and lack motivation in life.

Parents' Conditional Love

While love and continual affirmation are essential for a child's development and self-esteem, they become troublesome if parents display them seldom. A youngster shouldn't be denigrated for placing second, third, or fourth in class if they get praise for placing first. When parents instill in their children the idea that they must always succeed in order to be ahead of others and that failing is completely undesirable, they start to feel that their value is wholly dependent on their accomplishments. So it follows that such a person is someone who is always pursuing power, beauty, success, and renown. The trap of constantly becoming the greatest prevents them from ever discovering their actual selves. They never get the opportunity to encounter losses and disappointments in a constructive manner. It's as if you want to be the most knowledgeable person or you're a complete loser. There isn't a neutral position. Therefore, when someone develops the habit of receiving continual, even phony, praise and adulation to fuel their self-esteem, they cease empathizing with others.

Parental Narcissism and Children's Behavior

Additionally, a person's parents may unintentionally instill narcissism in them. Even if one of the parents exhibits manipulative, arrogant, or insensitive tendencies, the kid is likely to imitate such traits as they become older. A youngster is more likely to do the same if they are raised in an atmosphere where making fun of and demeaning other people is normal. When a kid grows up and becomes an adult, their conduct, the language they use, how they treat one another and other people, their choices in many areas, and their goals in life are all reflected in that child's later life.

Continuous evaluation and comparison

Then there are kids who are raised in a home where they are constantly compared to and criticized by others. When their kids can't live up to their expectations in any particular situation (which happens fairly often), one or both of the parents will make them feel humiliated, inadequate, and foolish. If there are many kids, they are all put up against one another. The youngster who today receives nothing but love and affection could tomorrow be completely crushed. Because the parents in such a household are often irate and furious and are not aware of their children's emotional needs, no youngster in the family experiences love in a stable and consistent way. Because of this, as such youngsters grow up, they persistently work to demonstrate that they are more than capable, despite the fact that their inner selves are constantly criticizing them.

Safeguarding Parents

Overly protective parents may foster narcissism in their kids by preventing them from making their own errors and learning from them. Some parents love their kids so much that they don't even notice when they behave badly. Such kids start to think that their wrongdoings are intended to be their power, and they may use it anytime they want. Instead, authoritative parenting promotes a child's development into a more independent and well-adjusted person.

A balanced method of parenting is authoritative parenting. Such parenting entails establishing boundaries and disciplining a kid while still being attentive, encouraging, and caring. Because their parents appreciate even their opinions and curiosity, children are never confused about anything. They get a fair response if they ask a question. They are told why something should be done or not done in order for children to understand what is morally appropriate and inappropriate.

Choosing The Right Words To Use

You've pursued your separation decision. Currently, you want to set up a respectable time to speak, as well as a strategy that is respectful, equitable, unambiguous, and nice. Breakups involve more than just planning your words. You should also think about how you would phrase it.

Here are some examples of things you may say. Use these ideas and modify them to suit the situation and fashion:

Let your BF or GF know that you need to talk about something important.

To start, state something positive or admirable about the other person.

For instance, "I truly like you and I'm glad we've become more acquainted with one another" or "We've become so acquainted with one another and I've come to value you."

Mention the issues that led to the breakup (your explanation for it).

For instance: But you later cheated on me, and I don't take that kind of thing seriously.

Or: We quarrel much more often than we have fun.

Alternatively, it no longer feels correct.

Suppose you now want to split up.

For instance: At the end, what I'm trying to communicate is that we should stop our relationship.

Or: Making friends is better for us than going out.

If it hurts, say you're sorry.

For example: I really don't want to harm you.

Or: If this isn't how you would have liked things to be, then please accept my apologies.

Or, I realize it would be challenging to hear this.

Say something pleasant or encouraging.

In this case, I have every confidence that everything will be well.

Or: I'll think back on our fun moments often.

Or: I am aware of another young man who would welcome the chance to go out with you.

Pay careful attention to what your spouse needs to say at this stage. Be patient and don't be shocked if the other person seems annoyed or unsatisfied with what you stated.

Give the person some room. Consider returning to a cordial exchange that shows your ex that you are interested in learning about how they are faring.

The Serious And Long-Lasting Consequences Of Living In A Narcissistic Society

Psychological Disorders

Echoism and mental health problems are both brought on by narcissistic abuse. People who have experienced this abuse often struggle to live, which strains their mental health. Since they are always under stress, cortisol, adrenaline, and norepinephrine are continually produced in response to their needs. They can never completely unwind because they are always aware of how precariously they are balancing on life, which they actually are doing.

Due to the narcissist's unpredictable nature and propensity for aggressive and abusive behavior, the victim learns to be vigilant and constantly look out for warning signals that the narcissist could erupt once again. The victim believes that the only way to prevent an explosion is to give in to the narcissist's every demand.

People who experience this form of abuse are more likely to have anxiety, codependency, depression, and often post-traumatic stress disorder.

Those who have experienced narcissistic abuse may wonder whether they are capable of having an accurate perception of reality. They typically have low self-esteem and believe that their needs and desires are insignificant and must be sacrificed for the narcissist. They do not recognize their worth and instead give in to sadness while living in continual fear of the next act of abuse by the narcissist.

Suicidal or self-harming thoughts

All of those mental health conditions raise the likelihood of self-harm and suicidal ideation. Some narcissistic abuse victims would consider suicide or self-harm as a coping mechanism because they are overworked and mistreated by the narcissist, frightened to breathe without permission, and certain that nothing will ever get better. In particular, if they feel stuck with no way out, such as if they lack a support system or access to the means to leave, they may feel as if they have no other alternative than to commit suicide as a relief from the narcissist's abuse.

Self-harm doesn't necessarily include cutting or leaving wounds; it may also involve self-medication and eating disorders. To relieve the tension caused by the narcissist, the victim may resort to drugs or alcohol, regularly drinking too much or looking for addictive and deadly substances. Such self-harm may lead to addiction, bodily ailments, injuries, or even death. The sufferer will risk developing a significant addiction in the future to get that brief, although hazardous, relief from the agony and numbness because the release they experience at the time seems worthy.

The Characteristics of Narcissistic Abuse Victims

Narcissistic abuse victims often exhibit a number of characteristics that are similar to those of narcissists and codependents. It is not usually the case that the codependent and the abuse victim are the same. Remember that not every abuse victim will exhibit all or all of these characteristics, and in some cases, a person who exhibits some of these characteristics has never experienced any kind of mistreatment or abuse. Do not take this information as gospel truth; rather, use it as a broad guide on what to look for in cases of abuse.

Dissociation

When the sufferer begins to separate themselves from any emotional state, dissociation takes place. The victim retreats inside himself or herself because it becomes easier to remain hidden behind a mask of numbness than to confront the abuse. This is a typical symptom of post-traumatic stress disorder or those who have experienced trauma. While striving to survive a short-term or acute trauma, this is helpful, it is not a condition that is good to maintain over the long run. Nobody will live a numb and detached life and be content or healthy.

Distrustful

It is simple to develop mistrust when abused and manipulated people are all around you. While you could still believe the narcissist, for example if he is gaslighting you and making you question who you are, you start to lose faith in both your capacity to comprehend the outside world and your capacity to believe in other people. Even if you manage to leave the narcissist, you can find it difficult to trust others or be vulnerable in new relationships. You could find it simpler to live in denial than to face the abuse head-on, mistrusting anybody who would try to express any form of concern about your situation.

Fearful

You could develop dread as a result of being subjected to narcissistic abuse in addition to mistrust. You've learned to be on guard all the time, wondering about the narcissist's response, how other people could interpret his reactions, and what will happen to you as a result of his explosive outbursts and propensity to overreact. This dread causes your body to continuously produce stress chemicals, making it impossible for you to ever completely rest.

Paranoid

You could develop paranoia as a result of a mixture of mistrust and dread. You believe that you lack objectivity or are unable to view things properly. You start to feel suspicious that others are attempting to manipulate you or are taking advantage of you, even though this is usually true of no one except the narcissist. The narcissist can be saying in your ear that anybody who speaks ill of the narcissist just wants him for themselves and that other people are just envious of what the two of you have.

Self-sacrificing

The narcissist expects his victims to completely give in to his whims, accommodating him whenever required and forgoing their own demands. You often act in this way as a coping technique to appease the narcissist, but with time you come to realize how irrelevant your own needs are. Instead of finding purpose and momentary relief in meeting the narcissist's needs because you understand that a content narcissist is a narcissist who is less likely to lash out at you, you eventually give up on them altogether after experiencing prolonged periods of being unable to assert yourself or meet your own needs. Of course, such happiness is fleeting.

Accusing Oneself

You could feel guilty about it at this time and blame yourself. You absorb this, particularly in light of the stereotype that victims of abuse are to blame for their situation and the narcissist's ear-to-ear whispers to that effect. You could feel that you might have used your strength or intelligence to flee the abuse before it became violent. You can believe that you are to blame for the abuse because of your own negligence or inadequacy. You can believe that you are innately undeserving of love. Despite the fact that abuse is never the victim's responsibility, you may find yourself placing the blame within in an effort to make sense of the circumstance.

Self-sabotaging

You could even start criticizing yourself to the point of self-sabotage. Because of the harm and distortion done to your self-esteem, you take the narcissist's assertions about your value at face value. You start to behave appropriately. For instance, if you cannot cook well enough, you can quit caring and decide it is not important. As a result, you may not bother to measure your ingredients carefully since the results would be subpar. In a more extreme example, you can internalize the idea that you can't make enough money to support yourself, which prevents you from pursuing professions that would bring you enough money to live on. You stay reliant on the narcissist because you never look for employment that enable you to live independently.

safeguarding their abuser

The need to fiercely defend the abuser may be the one feature that all abuse victims have in common. The victim is probably going to defend the abuser since they often still have feelings of loyalty or affection for the narcissist. If someone tells you that the abuser is not a good person, you may choose to counter with all the ways you see the abuser as a good person, such as mentioning how he took you on a nice vacation and showered you with love when you were in the idealization stage of your relationship. You may also choose to deny that the abuse was as severe as it may have been. This is sufficient for the sufferer, but people in the victim's immediate vicinity may see that the connection is unhealthy or abnormal.

Having Come To From a Nightmare:

Why It Would Be a Waste of Life To Spend It With Certain People

When did you first realize how valuable life is? Do you really need to undergo a near-death experience to comprehend this? The fact that no one is aware of life outside of the human existence should serve as your one wake-up call. Furthermore, until we pass away, the number of our days in this world is fixed, and nobody really knows what the future holds. That alone should serve as a reminder to appreciate your existence and being a person. The finest thing you can do is to live in the present since you won't live forever.

You should strive to love yourself and not give anything a chance in your life that can jeopardize your tranquility if you want to make it meaningful. You should declutter your life as one of the major concepts. Yes. You could already have gathered much more than you need in your life. It's possible that you've already let poison and negativity into your life and that you're holding so much that you don't believe you can let it go. What do you do, though? Will you continue to wriggle about in the same muck that you did in the past? The response would be "no" if you enjoy your life. Say "No" if anything disturbs you. De-cluttering doesn't only mean clearing out the physical clutter from your home. It covers a wide range of topics, such as ending poisonous relationships and phony friendships. Appreciate the ones who support you and let the others go. You don't have to please everyone on your trip, and you can't. Even those you believed loved you may abandon you due to the various distractions in today's environment, and they could even be purposefully taking advantage of you. However, be aware that those that are genuine and loyal to you won't desert you or purposefully use you.

A sad existence has many reasons, but one of the biggest is a poisonous relationship. When you are together, it not only prevents you from having peace of mind, but it also throws your life off balance after you have parted ways with your oppressor. Most people worry too much about little matters, so try not to worry too much. Remind yourself that life is very valuable and that nothing unimportant should occupy your time. Cutting back on these trivial matters will free up your attention to concentrate on the important things, such as improving your career, your relationships with important family and friends, and determining whether you are dating your perfect match or the wrong person. Nobody is so significant that they should enter your life with the sole purpose of making you unhappy. To recognize what each person is bringing into your life, you must be ready to meet them head-on when they arrive.

The worst things you can do in today's dating world are to seem desperate rather than assertive. You can't allow yourself to be in need. This will lead you to believe that someone is entering your life to "fill in a blank hole," and that is the source of all your suffering. You alone are in the best position to handle the problems in your life. The only person who really comprehends you is you. You are your own best supporter and the only one who can watch out for you. Your family is there to support and assist you in whatever you do up until you reach maturity, but then you are expected to take responsibility for your own actions. Every action you perform has a result of its own. The good news is that by refusing to let other people's ideals and beliefs occupy space in our minds and hearts, we can always learn to reduce the negative impact of those who do not wish us well and even insulate ourselves from such influence.

Your life ought to be in your hands. Starting now, you should determine for yourself what you want to take with you and what you want to leave behind. Finding your purpose in life should be your ultimate objective, and living a life that is in line with that purpose enables you to be happy and content. Remember that living a meaningful life takes careful preparation, taking responsibility for your own choices, and being prepared to defend yourself. You are in the greatest position to lead a fulfilling life if you are aware of where you are in life, where you want to go, and what you need to do to get there. Living in the moment to the fullest and not putting off tasks that are harmful to your welfare are the keys to leading a fulfilling life.

Keep in mind that your body is your greatest instrument for carrying out everyday activities, and your mind is your best tool for guiding your choices and daily chores. As a result, look after your emotional and physical health. Don't let someone squander time that might have been spent on things that matter to you in life. Recognize that each moment is important. Most essential, acknowledge your significance. No one has the right to tell you what to do since no one can do it better than you. Go for it if it would make you happy. Do not provide room in your life to someone who has an opposing viewpoint. Keep in mind that you are special and significant at all times.

Sometimes, particularly when dealing with a narcissist, the boundaries may become so hazy that you are unable to tell when someone has crossed them and is really in charge of your life, robbing you of the ability to live each day to the fullest and in a manner that is meaningful. As a result, keep an eye out for the following signs, which should alert you to the fact that you are somewhere you don't want to be.

You consistently complain about the same issue.

You should be aware of the general rule of thumb that if you have complained about anything two to three times, you are in a precarious situation. You must decide whether to accept it or modify it. If you're frustrated at work or with your relationship, you shouldn't see whining as anything more than a way to vent your irritation. This is an indication that you are intentionally rejecting something in life, not the opposite.

Your past is used to make you feel ashamed.

You can feel humiliated if you are often reminded of your prior failures. There are partners who are always willing to point out your prior faults. They help you to forget that your history only defines who you were, not who you are now or who you want to become. A toxic or narcissistic spouse will force you to talk about your history and will constantly exploit it to push you into a corner and give oneself more control. You will know you are in a bad position for your own growth and happiness when you begin to feel embarrassed of your history as a result of your partner's repeated reminders.

You've started to believe that changes are bad.

Adapting to change and taking advantage of opportunities as they arise are among the most important life concepts, particularly in the world of today. You should not engage someone who is swaying your view about changes or instilling fear of change in you since this is not the place for you. Change will get you where you want and need to go as long as you are making wise decisions.

Your Spouse Forced You to Give Up Your Favorite Hobbies

You feel delight whenever you complete a task that is essential to you. If you do action that makes you happy each day, you will know that you are moving in the correct way. However, this is not the best scenario for you to be in if your spouse criticizes your interests and makes you realize how wasteful or irrational they are. Nobody has the right to stand in the way of your pleasure.

You hardly ever have time to relax.

You want to demonstrate how much you can do in a day, yet you are always griping about how undervalued and worn out you are. We all have a total of 24 hours, some of which are set aside for sleeping so that you may refresh your thoughts before continuing with your task. If you don't get enough sleep, you're always angry and bitter. Such things gradually whisk your happiness and sanity away in unexpected ways.

You are not a superman who has to be always on the go. If you find yourself in this situation, you are likely attempting to appease your spouse because they have trained you to do so. Maybe your toxic spouse tries to keep you busy so you won't have a chance to free yourself from their influence. You obviously do not wish to live in such a situation and have a fulfilling life.

Disorder Of The Narcissistic Personality

Narcissism as a notion has a long history. The term of the personality condition, Narcissus syndrome, is derived from the ancient Greek story. In the late 1800s, narcissism was initially recognized by therapists as a mental disorder by physician Havelock Ellis. Narcissism was considered as a self-psychological theory by psychologist Sigmund Freud in the early 1900s (Pincus & Lukowitsky, 2009). But it wasn't until the early 1980s that narcissistic personality disorder gained widespread attention in the psychiatric community.

When diagnosing a client with narcissistic personality disorder, therapists use a number of processes. It is a mental ailment, hence a psychologist's knowledge is necessary.

This implies you should never give yourself a personality disorder diagnosis. You should first consult with your primary care physician so that you may address your concerns if you think you could be narcissistic. You will then be sent to a clinical psychologist from there. Although the traits of narcissism are discussed in this book, it is not a tool for self-diagnosis.

One of the many personality disorders included in the Diagnostic and Statistical Manual of Mental Disorders that therapists use to identify their patients with specific psychological diseases is narcissistic personality disorder. Although there is no treatment for narcissistic personality disorder, narcissists may acquire coping mechanisms via therapy that will enable them to improve their lives and those of their children. Naturally, they must admit they have a problem, which is quite difficult for someone with this disease to do. Many individuals may control their personality disorder using talk therapy and other techniques. They may maintain wholesome and solid bonds with their kids, significant others, friends, coworkers, and other members of the family.

Diagnostic Standards

Narcissistic personality disorder manifests in a variety of personality traits. This criteria will be used by your therapist to diagnose you, determine the form of narcissism you have, and assist you in creating a treatment plan. According to the DSM-IV and DSM-5 Criteria for the Personality Disorders (2012), five or more of the following characteristics must be present in order for someone to be diagnosed with narcissistic personality disorder.

Sense of Self-importance that is too big

Narcissistic people have a genuine sense that they are the center of the universe. Not even their kids can compare to how essential they are. They have such a strong sense of self-importance that they don't think they need to put in the effort to accomplish their objectives. Due to their importance and uniqueness, their objectives need to be fulfilled automatically. Additionally, they anticipate being acknowledged as a significant individual.

Feeling of Strong Entitlement

If you've ever heard the expression "born with a silver spoon in your mouth," you may relate to those who feel entitled. Being narcissistic is strongly correlated with this trait. They feel that because of who they are, they should be treated better than other individuals. They have to own the greatest residences, newest vehicles, and other goods.

Lack of Compassion

Empathy is the ability to comprehend another person's feelings. People who are narcissists lack empathy. While some people may display empathy in certain circumstances, it is often because they have other goals in mind. They can be coercing someone into doing what they desire. They might also be a more subdued or sensitive narcissist. However, all narcissists think that their emotions are what matter the most.

Utilize others' vulnerabilities

Narcissists will manipulate others to achieve their goals. If they want to, they can behave like your best buddy. This doesn't imply that they are your closest friend. It simply implies that you can provide them with what they want, whether you already have it or can get it on their behalf.

They Think They Are Special

Narcissists think they should only be friends with unique individuals like themselves. They feel that they should only associate with individuals who are on their level since anybody else won't be able to relate to them.

They Feel Jealous

A narcissist's envy might take one of two forms. Either they feel others are jealous of them or they are envious of other individuals. A narcissist usually envies others for their material things. They think that since they are superior and others desire to be like them, they are the ones who are envied.

They Dream of Being Powerful

Narcissists dream about a variety of things, including having boundless power and prosperity. Despite the fact that they could seem to be the greatest, they are aware that better individuals exist. There are some with more success or power. The narcissist fantasizes about having this kind of power because that is what they really want. They also have fantasies of becoming the smartest, most attractive, or a role model.

People must venerate them

When given the greatest attention and need for continual adoration, narcissists are happy. They think they should be elevated in the eyes of others.

It is difficult to interpret the narcissistic personality disorder criteria. Regardless matter whether you are the son or daughter of a narcissistic parent, it may be challenging to immediately recognize personality characteristics. You need to realize that these are just symptoms of a personality problem, regardless of who you are. They don't make up who a person is. The Diagnostic and Statistical Manual of Mental Disorders, the manual used by psychologists to identify mental diseases like Narcissistic Personality Disorder, may really be used to identify a mental ailment that applies to each and every one of us. For instance, you may be diagnosed with this guidebook if you suffer from anxiety, depression, or a learning handicap.

Do not let the criteria you just read cause you to lose faith, erupt in rage, or feel irritated. Use it as a tool to better understand yourself or your mother instead. Allow yourself to accept the requirements so that you may take charge of your own emotions and start building good connections.

Narcissistic personality disorder causes

Nobody completely comprehends the causes of narcissistic personality disorder. Narcissistic personality disorder has several underlying causes, including trauma experienced as a kid and other mental diseases. Genetics may be one explanation, according to many psychologists, although research into this is still in its early stages. In fact, there are so many reasons that they cannot all be included in this book's pages. This is due to the fact that each individual is unique. Therefore, each narcissistic mother had various life events and elements that contributed to the development of this personality condition. We'll look at a few of the most well-known causes in this section.

Causes in Early Childhood

Sometimes having a narcissistic parent as a child causes someone to acquire narcissistic personality disorder. Not every kid of a narcissistic parent will go on to have a personality problem, though. However, parents are where kids pick up social and behavioral clues. This raises the possibility that you may experience a kind of narcissistic personality disorder at some point in your life. Other potential contributing factors from childhood include insensitive parenting, harsh criticism, parental neglect, excessive pampering and overpraise, trauma, and abuse.

One of the most researched causes of narcissistic personality disorder is childhood maltreatment. According to many studies, a kid is four times more likely to acquire a personality disorder if their mother verbally abuses and neglects them (Burgemeester, n.d.).

Examining your early years and learning to face the main cause is one method to start controlling your narcissistic personality if you believe it may be a result of them. Even though it won't be simple, if you don't take this step, you'll have trouble managing the personality disorder. Taking on the problem's root is one of the finest methods to regain control. Utilize this opportunity to become a stronger person rather than allowing yourself to be afraid of your past. A strong person is someone who can control their fear and strive to improve both their own and other people's lives. This power is within of you.

Genetic Roots

Studies on genetic factors are still in their early stages. But researchers have found a gene that is sometimes referred to as "the selfish gene." According to Burgemeester (n.d.), this gene is thought to be one of the underlying causes of narcissistic personality disorder. It is crucial to keep in mind that more study on this gene is still necessary in order to determine if there is a hereditary component to narcissistic personality disorder or whether all of its causes are environmental.

Narcissism Types

There are two primary categories of narcissistic moms. The first kind are narcissists who envelop others ("Characteristics of Narcissistic Mothers", n.d.). These are the moms that meddle too much in your affairs. You are seen by them as a continuation of yourself. She often fails to recognize you as an individual. They deeply ingratiate themselves into your life. For instance, when it comes to enveloping moms, there are no restrictions. Since newborns and toddlers don't yet comprehend limits, this could be okay for them, but as the kid gets older, it will become quite difficult.

The mother will often discover that her kid is attempting to create their own identity. The mother will get aggressive very soon if this occurs. She will attempt to influence her kid to behave in a certain manner and do what she wants. In order to foster empathy in her kid, the mother will also exploit her child's emotions. When the youngster disobeys their mother's instructions, this empathy will be exploited to make them feel guilty.

According to "Characteristics of Narcissistic Mothers", n.d., the ignoring kind of narcissistic mother is the second type. These moms resemble the enveloping narcissist nearly exactly. They are able to distinguish clearly between themselves and their kids. They observe them so closely, in fact, that they often ignore their own children. They seldom ever express interest in the lives of their kids. When they do, it's often because they stand to benefit from it. For instance, if their kid is getting an award, the mother would attend the event just to use it as an opportunity to promote herself. Since she was the one who raised the child, the only reason the kid received the prize was because she was such a fantastic mom.

In addition to these two sorts of narcissistic moms, there is also the type who is covertly cruel. At least in the eyes of her children, this woman seems to have two personalities. She will portray the kind mother who loves her children while she is out in public. She will treat her children cruelly, however, when she is alone in her house. To obtain what she wants, she will say cruel things or treat people unfairly in various ways. There is also a mother who is emotionally fragile.

While the majority of narcissists thrive on emotional neediness, others may utilize it to boost their self-esteem. If a woman feels she needs anything emotionally, she may seek to her kid to provide for her financially or in any other manner that may satisfy her needs.

What Is Narcissistic Abuse

There are many different types of abuse, and the great majority of them never even leave the victim with a physical mark. The victim still suffers at the hands of the abuser regardless of the many types of abuse that are used. Whatever its form, this kind of behavior is unacceptable and should never be permitted. The overwhelming sense of loneliness you experience again and over again is the earliest and most telling clue to yourself that you are in a poisonous relationship with a narcissist. It's possible that you are dealing with a narcissist who is only showing you a mirage of the relationship you thought you were living if you see your boyfriend every day when you get home, share meals with him, watch TV with him, and then go to bed next to him but still feel alone. Underneath the acts that leave you feeling bewildered, confused, and very lonely, there is an absence of emotion. It may be an indication of narcissistic abuse syndrome if you experience this on a regular basis and are unaware of where the sensation comes from.

The Dangerous Attraction between a Narcissist and an Empath

A person who empathizes feels intensely both their own feelings and those of others. They are the folks who, whether at work or school, respond quickly and strongly to both good and negative news that their friends and loved ones share with them. In their careers as therapists or in other medical fields, some empaths utilize their empathy to benefit others. Others could have a little sense of weightiness as they strive to manage their lives while bearing the emotions of others around them. Everyone has encountered someone who fits the description of an empath. When you're pleased, upset, or wherever in between, they can relate and feel it. They are a lot of fun to celebrate with since joy rapidly spreads to the empath and is contagious.

Now, this very compassionate and sensitive individual meets a narcissist by chance. When she is among her pals, it may happen at a restaurant or pub. He hears bits and pieces of her talks with others around and notices that she cares profoundly about them, participating in their suffering and doing all she can to assist. She could see her comforting a friend at a coffee shop while acting nearly as distraught as the friend who had the breakup, or in another circumstance.

Narcissistic Abuse Types

Physical Neglect

When most people contemplate abuse, they picture this. Physical punishments are a kind of physical abuse. Physical abuse is anything that causes physical injury to your body, whether or not it leaves a mark on you. It is considered physical abuse and should not be accepted if the other person ever touched you in any manner without your permission or at a time when you did not want to be touched. In the end, you have control over your body, and you have the right to determine whether or not you want to be touched.

Language Abuse

You are verbally abused each time the voice is used in a manner that is intended to harm or belittle you. This covers hurtful statements like belittling, derogatory remarking, or shouting at you. The narcissist uses his voice to keep you down, but other individuals may say critical things but utilize them legitimately to help you improve. Verbal abuse often goes unnoticed because it does not physically harm you, but enduring continual name-calling or insults may wear you down and create long-term harm to your mental health.

Threats, demands, guilt trips, sarcasm, shouting, calling people names, insults, and any other verbal injury that you deem to be purposeful and damaging are all considered forms of verbal abuse.

sexual assault

Sexual abuse, which includes forced sexual actions or sexual contact without permission, is one of the most pernicious, harmful types of abuse that can be inflicted onto another person. Even just stroking you in a manner that makes you feel uncomfortable or tapping your butt without your permission would be seen as sexual assault; there is no need that this include complete intercourse.

Keep in mind that just though you may be dating or married to the other person, that individual does not have the right to utilize your body in ways that make you uncomfortable. If it is not voluntary, a spouse may sexually abuse the other person. Keep in mind that neither a person who is sleepy nor someone who is under the influence of drugs or alcohol can agree to sexual contact. The act of pressuring you into having sex you do not want is also seen as sexual abuse.

Abuse of money

You are in some way prevented from accessing money if you are a victim of financial abuse. This is especially prevalent in abusive couples, while it isn't always the case, one person often remains at home and makes all the money. Regardless of who makes the money, one person seizes control of it all and limits access to it. The whole purpose is to keep the victim trapped, depending on the abuser to provide all of their requirements.

This is often accomplished by limiting access via the use of various bank accounts, giving the victim either nothing at all or just modest sums of money at a time to pay essential expenses while withholding the rest. The abuser may have used theft to seize control of your finances, removed your access to money and restricted it, or simply moved all of your money into an account that you are not allowed to access. Another way to accomplish it is to get credit cards in your name and use them to rack up debt and keep you ensnared. Financial abuse may occur if both partners in a marriage do not have equal access to the money and have not consented to that arrangement. Some couples decide to divide their money, but this must be a mutual choice.

Emotional Violence

As the term indicates, emotional abuse aims to cause you emotional harm. Threats to keep you in line, the silence treatment, making fun of you, or the preferred love bomb and devaluation cycle, also known as the FOG, are all examples of this. Your emotions are being played with for no other reason than to amuse the narcissist. The majority of manipulation efforts fall under this category since they try to influence you by playing on your emotions.

Isolation

Isolation is the deliberate restriction of contact with those who may provide the sufferer with help. This involves dissuading others from contacting the victim, such as by making it awkward for the victim's friends and relatives to visit so that they finally refuse to do so, or by limiting social media communication. The narcissist is probably isolating you if they demand that you cut off particular individuals if you want to keep the relationship going.

Symptoms of a Narcissistic Relationship

You gradually start to show obvious indicators of an abuse victim when you are continually exposed to certain sorts of abuse. Not every individual will behave in exactly the same way or display every single symptom on the list, and the absence of any one of these signs does not always rule out abuse. So that you can spot abuse in yourself or others, familiarize yourself with this list.

The warning indicators listed below will assist you in identifying the painful connection brought on by being in a narcissistic relationship.

Your voice has been muted.

Your voice is often muffled by narcissists since they only care about their own voice, particularly if you are an empath. It may not begin violently at first, but over time you will notice that your opinions and feelings are no longer important and that this charismatic character has taken control of your life, leaving you with no say whatsoever. Because you are no longer the same person you used to be, your friends and family who are keen observers will believe you are behaving "strange" because you have lost your voice.

An Illusion of a Relationship

It is simpler for you to defend the person's flaws and create an inaccurate picture of your relationship when you are dating a narcissist. The abuse and poisonous behavior will be easier to tolerate if you convince yourself that you are not suffering in the relationship, even while others can see that you are.

Controlling and manipulative behavior

A narcissist is not only self-centered; they also try to manipulate people to control their behavior since it is the only way they can maintain control over everyone else and maintain their dominance.

Bottled and persistently negative emotions

Because the whole relationship is designed to feed this person's ego, his ideas, and everything else that is focused on them, you won't ever have the luxury of speaking your mind while you are with a narcissist.

When feelings are suppressed for an extended period of time, a person becomes less emotionally expressive, which leads to the emergence of doubts, worries, phobias, and poor self-confidence, which finally destroy the person's faith in the connection.

You experience sadness or depression a lot.

You should feel content in a healthy relationship. It may be time to look closely at why you are feeling this way if you regularly experience sadness and depression in a relationship and these sentiments cannot be linked to anything external to your connection. Even if you are unable to identify the abusive behaviors, you may be able to understand how you feel. The despair and melancholy you experience might be the consequence of emotional abuse.

Self-blame and guilt

You could even start to blame yourself for the violence, telling yourself that since you irritated your abuser and they punched you, it won't happen again if you are more cautious in the future. Making yourself accountable for the narcissist's conduct simply makes you believe that the abuse was acceptable since you were to blame for it.

Your pride in your achievements has decreased.

The narcissist will downplay your successes while highlighting their own. It may be a clue of the narcissistic abuse you have experienced if you notice that things that used to make you joyful or proud no longer do so. The issue with this kind of abuse is that you could unconsciously like your spouse, making it difficult for you to recognize language that denigrates you for the abuse that it is. Just remember that your spouse should improve your self-esteem, not worsen it.

putting reality into doubt

One of the narcissist's main objectives is to keep you bound to their idealized version of reality, and in order to do this, they must keep you cut off from what reality really is. This leads to the person living a life where the actual truth is that everyone else is leading a life you find dubious. You'll realize that you're perplexed.

It almost has a love triangle vibe to it.

The narcissist might torment you even more than before by introducing a third party dynamic into the relationship and forming a love triangle. By doing this, the abuser may spread the notion that the victim is unworthy. The victim then strives to receive the love and attention they need, and you constantly try to attract the narcissist's attention in order to acquire what you want.

Although a part of you wants to end the relationship, you are too afraid to do so.

When one experiences violence in a relationship, it is only normal to desire to end it. The abused person always choose when or if to leave, but they often talk themselves out of leaving or are too afraid to go. It may be a clue that you are interacting with an abusive narcissist if you often consider ending the relationship but feel unable to do so.

Loneliness

You will always feel lonely if you are in a relationship with a narcissist, which is another drawback. The individual may still be in your relationship, but because of how self-absorbed they are, you will feel alone most of the time.

Because you tend to desire to be alone all the time, feeling lonely when connected to someone else might be emotionally devastating. The loneliness you experience with a narcissist is especially painful since, despite being made aware of your situation, he will do nothing to help.

You experience unjustified fatigue.

You can feel worn out by the narcissist's emotional assault. Relationships with them may be rather emotional whirlwinds, and the most obvious sign of this journey is simply that you feel worn out. You may experience exhaustion that cannot be adequately explained by anything else if you are dating a narcissist.

You are acting in a manner that is not in your best interests.

A narcissist might influence you to make decisions that are in your best interests rather than your own. They act in this manner because they do not see your needs as being equivalent to their own, nor do they view you as being generally equal to them. You should take a hard look at your relationship if you discover that you only behave in the narcissist's best interests.

You discover falsehoods spoken by your partner

Pathological liars may include narcissists. They fabricate because they have desires and "needs" that can only be satisfied by deception. For instance, a narcissist may need your money, attention, or other things and may have to lie to you to acquire them. The falsehood enables them to get the needs and wants that would otherwise be denied if their partner had been acting rationally. In fact, the narcissist's whole identity is often a fake.

Dissociating or Detaching

You may disconnect from your emotions via the coping technique called dissociation. Your emotions might sometimes be so intense for you that you believe you have to completely separate from them in order to live. This is typically seen in survivors of traumatic events like rape or war, as well as in narcissistic abuse victims. When this happens, your mind is seeking to isolate the abuse since that is the only way it is aware of how to deal with it. If left unchecked, this may lead to some major mental health issues. It may result in altered states of consciousness, the beginning of memory loss, as well as catastrophic health consequences.

Never Trust Anyone

You may respond by becoming highly wary after seeing so much abuse from someone you previously liked and trusted. Your capacity to form lasting connections may decrease as a result of your persistent anxiety of being misled or injured again. Instead, you continue to be too cautious around others, which only helps to amplify anxiety-related feelings and create barriers between you and them. After your experience, you probably begin to worry that someone you have never had cause to dislike may hurt you.

Frequently or Always afraid

You may find yourself continually dreading a repetition of the abuse as a consequence of feeling so completely misled. If you have managed to flee your abuser, you may worry that they will find you again or that any pleasure you have is a mirage. You've probably experienced penalties for enjoying life on several occasions since narcissists prefer to punish when those around them are pleased, which has only served to increase your anxiety whenever things go well. You live in continual terror that the narcissist will be triggered or that the other shoe would drop, shattering your little moment of enjoyment. You could grow to dread pleasure and, as a result, enable the narcissist to continue being the only one to take pleasure in anything. The narcissist takes pleasure in seeing his victims struggle to enjoy life.

Self-sabotaging

When you self-sabotage, you look for methods to hinder your own success. This often has to do with the narcissist eroding your self-esteem. You start to act out the narcissist's claims about your skills because you start to believe them.

If you are told that you are stupid over and over again, you will start to believe it and start acting accordingly. Regardless matter how intelligent you are, your decisions will be influenced by how you feel about yourself. Self-sabotage may also take the shape of not taking the required actions to give yourself the independence you want, so making it hard for you to quit the relationship when you want to.

Understanding Anxiety And Depression Disorders Of The Mind

often attempt to seek assistance only because they are not feeling well. These folks are often fairly normal people who are merely battling a predisposition to be depressed or suffering with life, overreacting with concern to different circumstances or occurrences, and so forth. However, borderline and narcissistic individuals often have little awareness of their lack of accountability. Instead, they will blame others for not accepting responsibility. Anyone married to such a person would understand how weird and difficult this is to cope with.

Now let's take a closer look at both borderline and narcissistic personality disorders. We'll look at the symptoms as well as potential treatment options for the patient's spouse.

Always Putting the Blame on Others

Regarding this behavior, there is never any relief. A narcissist is never at fault, and as a result, they are never to blame for anything.

They have no notion of accepting responsibility for one's actions. One that they don't want to get to know.

On the other hand, you will unquestionably be held responsible for everything.

And to make matters worse, there are times when everything goes wrong for everyone. It is known as life. This placing of blame on others arises from the fact that someone must be held accountable for whatever went wrong. even if they had little to no involvement in what really transpired.

You are to responsible in this situation for lacking the insight to foresee and act quickly.

Therefore, even if you could not foresee anything, you are still to fault for lacking foresight.

The narcissist will be quick to criticize you for whatever shortcomings you may have. They are experts at projecting their own low self-esteem and lack of personal accountability onto other people. Also referred to as assigning blame.

Their own failure mostly goes undetected as long as they can get everyone's focus on someone else. They get a pretty bad habit out of it that they continue to engage in even when the persons they are blaming are not there. also quite effective.

It is much simpler when these folks are not there since they are unable to defend themselves.Additionally, they have a propensity to blame others for their unending bliss.

This is like magic because if they experience misery for whatever reason, even one that they have created for themselves, they always attribute it to you. This is because, despite everything else, you are obliged to keep them content at all times. Every time they express discontent, you have, in a sense, failed badly in your job.

When the occasion demands it, they transform you into the villain and make themselves the victim.

People mistakenly believe that after you leave these kinds of relationships, this behavior stops. Sadly, no, it doesn't. The only distinction is that once you leave, they won't directly blame you for anything.

Then, instead, they'll be disparaging you continuously behind your back. For this reason, it is often preferable to maintain your presence.

Making their improbable tales plausible becomes much more challenging for them when the individuals they typically communicate to are continually exposed to your character.

Therefore, you must understand that ending a relationship with a narcissistic person would be seen as an insult by them. In reality, you are berating them for not being good enough in your eyes.

They won't take this well since they are generally quite sensitive to criticism. They are unable to recognize your right to make your own decisions about what is best for you.

That if you stop choosing them, it's not personal and is just a case of "It just didn't work out between us." We all desire circumstances that make us feel good about ourselves and about life in general, just as they do. Just like that. The fact that you are not calling them rubbish by any means and would be lenient to having a platonic relationship with them, is something the Narcissistic individual who was an intimate partner doesn't want to entertain or comprehend. Considering that they really believe they are "perfect,"

Which thus makes their viewpoint completely logical.

What happens is that when you don't want to engage with them on a level they want you to, when you request that they treat you differently from before, preferably with some respect. Then you are calling them, "not good enough" as they are by default.

You are therefore naturally wrong and making them very angry at you in the process.

Once again, they are never to blame for anything that goes wrong, simply never. Even when you point out to them how they did indeed act wrongly according to the facts, they will agree begrudgingly but quickly tell you that they had no choice.

They immediately point the finger at someone else who presumably forced them or at unavoidable circumstances. It is the classic copout used by them to always avoid taking personal responsibility for anything.

How To Avoid And Manage A Narcissist

Techniques Used By Narcissists And How They Manipulate

Because of your prior experience, you are familiar with the attributes and characteristics of narcissists. It is well known that the narcissist is a manipulator. Along with their habit, they use a variety of other strategies to fulfill their objective. How to stay away from narcissists will be covered in this part.

But it's best to start with the methods and how they apply them to their bait. The lesson on how to avoid them will become profoundly clearer after being exposed to their methods.

to be more knowledgeable. I'll go through 15 original strategies used by narcissists.

1. Gaslighting. This is one of the traditional strategies a narcissist would use. There are several ways to explain this method. I'll explain this in three sentences. These include: That didn't occur. You're imagining things; are you insane?

Most experts currently agree that more explanation is one of the most cunningly manipulative strategies used in the field of narcissism. Its purpose is to determine how people's perceptions of reality are distorted. It makes it impossible to follow one's intuition and reach a logical conclusion. Additionally, when you feel unjustified, even when mistreated or abused, you often lack the skills necessary to loosen up and reject the ideas that are put out to you.

For instance, when a narcissist claims that it is all in your mind. They give you the impression that you are unable to grasp reality and that you have a skewed understanding of the reality that exists in the world of every person. or when they declare you to be insane. They constantly give you the impression that you are either mentally ill or lack morality.

2. Projection. You've seen that a poisonous narcissist would never acknowledge that he is solely to blame for the chaos going on around him. Instead, they can unfairly place the responsibility on you. A projection is the term used to describe that method. We are all guilty, even if you could have even

done it in the past. I can witness to that since I have.

But when it's done often, that's when it starts to become a habit. And those are the methods used by narcissists. It goes deeper than that, too.

By projecting, a person transfers blame for their unfavorable behaviors and qualities on someone else who is more familiar to them. Even someone else might be given the task. For instance, if somebody arrived late to a meeting, they would complain that the timing is bad and that it needs to be changed. They turn the tables instead of blaming themselves for their failure to reach the deadline. This tactic may give others who are close to these people the impression that they are unbalanced, unstable, and never accomplishing things well, even if this impression may not be factual.

3. Generalization. Anyone who has narcissistic tendencies will also use this strategy. Take this instance for a deeper understanding. Let's say you complained to a colleague at work about how he sometimes doesn't consider the long-term effects of personal choices. But the narcissist in the workplace insists that you called him a loose gun. You continue by warning him that things may get out of hand if they continue in this manner. However, your narcissistic coworker erupted and claimed that you labeled him a catastrophe.

Do we remark that he doesn't comprehend your target? No, he does, but he's intellectually too lazy. He generalizes problems rather than spending time analyzing the topic and seeing it from all angles. He says things like, "Whatever you say, and don't recognize the senses in your logical reasoning." He also won't take into consideration other viewpoints. He fails and would want to be an intellectual genius, even if you are thinking critically and making sure he uses his intelligence. And if you're not cautious, you can be forced to lie out of fear and even acknowledge the stereotype.

4. shifting the goals. This is a logical error, and Narcissists often use it. They do this to ensure that they have every excuse under the sun to be unhappy with you forever. And this occurs even when all the logical evidence supporting a certain assertion has been supplied. Or they do anything to accommodate their

wish. They keep asking you probing questions. In fact, in a different fashion, they could even ask you for further evidence, and by doing so, they have the freedom to assign responsibility.

Take, for instance, when you choose to act in accordance with company policy and you make every effort to meet the standard. They may criticize your attitude and claim that you haven't done anything noteworthy for the company, or you may need to support your claim with additional evidence. The more you strive to prove yourself, the more unworthy you feel and the more likely it is that everything you believe is incorrect for them. He will therefore succeed in his goal of lowering your self-esteem and making you dread them while doing your job.

5. Changing the subject. This narcissist strategy has been effective for a very long time. It is still in use today and hasn't stopped. Although you may assume there's no harm in changing the subject of a discussion, a manipulator will do it to get out of being held accountable or to avoid accepting blame for their conduct. They wouldn't want people to continue talking about anything that would hold them responsible for something. They will redirect the topic to their advantage in order to do that.

Unfortunately, if you are unconscious, this may continue indefinitely, and it will put a stop to the debate of important subjects. Also keep in mind that the more you engage in pointless discussion, the more you overlook the important ones, which makes it impossible for you to address the essential issues. Keep in mind that they are not really acting in your favor; rather, they are working against you. He points out your weaknesses and makes you feel more useless as the chat goes on. So the key to winning the battle against a narcissist is to remain focused on the underlying issue.

6. Calling with name. Although it could seem minor, I assure you that it is harmful. As subtle as it may be, it has the power to cut right through you, leaving you feeling unworthy and allowing you to call yourself all kinds of things. It may last indefinitely until you are unable to stand it any longer. You must thus put a stop to it.

They can start by calling you names because of something you did wrong. When it spreads around the globe, everyone begins to see you in that way; their first impression of you is based on your name, not the fact that it makes it harder for you to focus on your work. When this happens, you'll be worried about what other people will think and feel about what you do since their opinions will affect how you see yourself.

Another aspect of narcissism that name-calling exposes is that they are lacking in higher-level thinking skills. They want to use you as their playground so they may rule over your inferior state as a king. Unexpectedly, it may occur anywhere. Even in positions of authority in politics, it is possible.

7. Spitting campaigns. You may be aware that telling falsehoods is a characteristic of those who exhibit narcissistic behavior. But how can they apply this strategy to other people?

They start by attempting to change the way you perceive yourself. But what if that one is impossible to complete? The next thing they do is play the martyr, which causes them to classify you as poisonous. It has been determined that this effort is a preemptive attack that will be utilized to harm your reputation and guarantee that they smear you everywhere they meet.

Many groups may become divided as a result of the campaign; some may agree with the falsehoods, while others may contest them. And even among intelligent people, this may occur. Sad to say, if this affects you, it may also damage your reputation. Your status will continue to be in grave danger as a result.

They are so cunning that their slander campaign will first be taken seriously. They could highlight one of your flaws and paint a false picture of you, making it appear as if you've been engaging in that behavior for a very long period. They will prevail even if you don't intelligently contest their claim.

8. Devaluation. You're not new to this, but one thing about devaluation is that it

starts with love because the same individual who would falsely report on both you and the person who had the job you now hold will also falsely report on them. They can begin by praising you and seeming to understand the wisdom of what you've done in contrast to what the person in the position did.

Pick one as an example. When an employee behaved cruelly, the person in your position sometimes sanctioned or fired them. However, when something similar occurred during your tenure, you issued a stern caution and underlined that it should never happen again. Now, a narcissist may not be able to determine if one instance is more important than the others. They can begin to undervalue their former teammate in an effort to promote you. But if you start to believe it, they will use what they did to the former colleague against you. Yes, you won't have to question this again in the future.

9. A crude joke. We should all be able to laugh at ourselves. And a narcissist won't focus on this positive feeling of self. He would like to hide behind it and shoot off cutting quips that are hostile against the target.

For instance, a covert narcissist might enjoy making jokes about your integrity that were both explicit and nasty. They may then add "it's just a joke" after saying it, which will allow them to get away with expressing such abhorrent remarks. And even while they do it, they may maintain a composed and innocent demeanor. They will argue that you lack a reasonable sense of humor if you attempt to prove that such comments are improper and unhealthy. That is incorrect.

You could even wonder if what occurred was simply a little innocent fun when you think about it. It's an outright falsehood. The humor is rough. They're doing that to undermine your self-worth and get you to question your judgment. It is very prevalent among friends, particularly among colleagues. They could subject you to this. You must be able to recognize comedy that undermines your self-confidence and distinguish it from humor that is just amusing. Although it's rare, it might be an indication if the joke makes you feel bad.

10. Triangulation. This has shown to be one of the narcissists' most clever strategies. They want to draw your attention away from their weaknesses so that you may concentrate on the potential danger posed by another individual. Triangulation is what it is termed for this reason.

The methods include a passion for rebutting untruths regarding what others have stated about you. To get to this conclusion, the person they are reporting the statement to you to would have been duped. The individual isn't really your opponent; they're just a victim.

However, a narcissist could portray the individual as your adversary. Therefore, giving too much attention to what "they said" might make someone who has been "manipulated" into an opponent.

Who has been able to make it work? Triangulation tactics are being used by the narcissist to manipulate.

11. Shaming. We will never get all we want in life or in our way of living. And narcissists now use that reality as one of their play areas. They could start by pointing out your deficiencies. Use it to embarrass you. Let's look at two instances.

Your lack of a degree may appeal to a narcissist. Even if you have extensive exposure and experience, a narcissist may criticize your logic in a public setting where you and he are engaged in debate and humiliate you by pointing out that you lack a degree when, if you had one, you might have been able to see his point of view.

Another illustration is how you look. Do you tend to dress conservatively while not keeping up with the newest fashion trends? Your lack of taste in fashionable attire may irritate a narcissist who may use it against you.

The narcissist is always on the move to demean everybody who crosses their path and to see or hear anything that offends them in order to humiliate the person they are using it on.

12. Brainwashing. This is one of the psychological tricks that manipulators use, but narcissists are also masters of this art. Even if you may first insist that you won't do a certain chore or perform a certain obligation, you eventually catch yourself doing it. Your mind has been deceived.

They utilize deception to force you to follow orders even when you don't want to in order to accomplish this. For instance, they can begin by outlining the financial advantages of accepting this position. They can begin by citing instances of individuals who took advantage of opportunities without working hard and had significant economic impact. And all of this works in their favor; if you begin to follow their commands, before you realize it, you have turned into a pet that they are free to raise and lower as they like.

13. Unsuitable Actions. A narcissist often exhibited more outgoing behaviors. It has been noted that they often utilize more explicit terminology. Because of this, they often embarrass you in front of others. Additionally, you will need to

apologize to them for their unacceptable actions.

Additionally, that activity is being pushed at you so you may make them feel more important and bolster their ego. And if they strike out at you for that, you're more inclined to assist them make amends, which will allow them to get away with undesirable conduct.

Narcissistic conduct that is out of place is often insulting and may be damaging to your personality. They often use sexual terminology as a starting point to undermine your confidence. Before you realize it, you've been duped. One of the finest things to do in this situation is to recognize the direction a discussion is taking and the main driving force. You may avoid getting dragged into the discussion by paying attentively from the start and giving what is being said careful consideration. By removing yourself from that scenario, you could be doing yourself a favor and preserving your confidence.

14. lacking emotional self-control. Physical hostility might result from narcissists' inability to regulate their emotions. And in certain cases, they could start off by scaring you to make you feel afraid, then they might threaten you before finally resorting to using derogatory words. These words will be used against you to denigrate you. Is that where it ends?

Their outburst of rage can result in them withdrawing their support. This assistance might be material, emotional, or financial. They're doing this to give you the impression that an apparently bad conduct is harming them.

A narcissist may use this tactic by limiting your access to friends and family if you are in a relationship with them, such as if they are your husband or wife. They could even be the driving force behind your actions. Additionally, they'll exert a lot of pressure on you to do what you initially didn't want to do. A person may get scared as a result of this attitude, in which case he may need to know how to secure his safety. Additionally, this kind of assault might result in domestic violence, which can be traumatizing.

15. acting the victim. This should be mentioned since it is the narcissist's last tactic. This method has an attitude that will compel you to feel sorry for them so that their ego will be bolstered.

Deep down, they are aware of your firm attitude, which is why you often hear them complain, "I can't win with you." They'll be tempted to give in if you do this. You may then let them go and give them complete freedom.

Narcissists utilize these 15 strategies, among others. Today, everyone is out in full force—at work, at class, with family, and even among friends.

However, it is clear that you can prevent the issue and even have some control over their impact. That is, a portion of their influence on you. But how can you do this? In order to help you obtain therapy, I'd want to share with you how to look at your relationship and determine whether you have been a victim of this. These pointers will enable you to support your assertion and put things into perspective. They will also better position you to comprehend what you can do to prevent them.

Potential Roots Of Narcissism

Narcissism's true causes are not entirely understood by scientists. A home setting that is distinct from that of the "normal," healthy individual is what most psychological research indicate. Other times, the narcissist is impacted by certain personal events, which causes a compensatory behavior to emerge. A family that overprotects and spoils the kid might foster a strong feeling of entitlement that also leaves the familial context. As a result of their parents' reverence for them and their constant praise, whether justified or not, the individual now assumes that everyone will treat them like royalty. At the same time, an abusive environment may make it necessary to compel ego protection and assertion. Since the individual now inflates their own ego as a result of an entrenched practice of defending oneself against attack or diminution of their identity by family members, this might lead to the development of the narcissistic personality disorder. A youngster may also have NPD if their family is uncaring or inattentive since they grow up learning that there isn't much love in the world. The narcissist has the ability to focus their own love and attention on oneself. They have been socialized to believe that relationships are frivolous, selfish affairs, that individuals should behave like strangers and have no regard for others, etc.

Childhood personal experiences may have such a profound impact on someone that they end up developing NPD. For instance, a whole psychological complex is created if the individual has causes to feel inferior (to their peers). It is commonly recognized that having a superiority complex does not always entail that the individual experiencing it strongly believes they are better than other people. A person may develop a superiority complex as a coping strategy to deal with upsetting events. A secret and sneaky feeling of inferiority is often at the core of a superiority complex, according to psychologist Alfred Adler who conducted extensive research on this topic. This defense mechanism is founded on an effort to conceal, deny, and mask the inferiority complex. When narcissism develops as a result of these events, it serves a protective purpose. The narcissist had feelings of difference and inferiority in comparison to others at some time throughout their upbringing. Then came the second stage, when they were focused on establishing their supremacy and winning the respect of others. Thus, the narcissist was taught to act in a manner that may atone for whatever inferiority complexes they had in the past. When narcissism is already present, such sentiments are deeply buried in the person's subconscious, and when they do come to the surface, the narcissist primarily feels entitled to things and has an inflated view of themselves.

According to some experts, narcissism may also have genetic and psychobiological reasons. If this is true, narcissists would be less accountable for their disease because their abnormal behaviors would have their roots in the brain rather than their behavior. But while a number of elements may combine to cause narcissism, the most important ones are probably socio-psychological rather than hereditary or biological. You should assume that a number of elements are entwined for such a complex condition to form while researching someone you believe to be a narcissist. Narcissism is likely the result of a method of conditioning, but genetics may also be involved if a predisposition to feel superior to others and a feeling of self-importance run in the family. There can also be hereditary characteristics at work. But let's not forget that people can typically manage their own personalities and choose whatever traits they wish to develop or not. Instead than rationalizing the narcissist with a reference to heredity, the focus should be on understanding the probable reasons of narcissism and looking into a person's background.

Relationship With A Narcissist

Many people are unaware of the dangers that come with having a self-centered accomplice. It's everything but a pleasant relationship with everyone since egotists are self-centered, destructive, manipulative, and they subject their victims to a variety of fervent forms of extortion and pain.

Narcissistic Personality Disorder has negative consequences on others since these individuals lack empathy and a true understanding of others' emotions. Additionally, dealing with self-centered partners may be quite confusing since they might be kind to you one day and betray you the next. They often have a hard time deciding whether to love you or hate you. Because of this, a lot of people who are close to egomaniacs watch it and attempt to understand their constant display of hot and cold affection.

We shall examine the behavior of the egotist while receiving admiration in greater detail in this section. This can help you determine if your partner is an egotist and whether you are really motivated to leave this toxic relationship.

The Narcissist Love Circle

The majority of the time, it is often too late to recognize that you are working with an egomaniac. A complete separation becomes problematic in this way. Some people might have spent a considerable amount of time with the egomaniac before getting married and having children. In spite of all the trauma they may have sustained from being in a relationship with a narcissist, some people also get attached to it and reliant.

In fact, some people may even come to the realization that they aren't good enough for greater things and don't deserve the best due to the various egotistical conspiracies. These people have been treated badly and made to feel worthless repeatedly, and over time they start to believe it themselves.

A Narcissist Loves in What Way?

When in love, the egomaniac behaves in a way that is distinct from how other people behave. Below, we shall look into their display of love in order to draw attention to it. Throwing Lures

They are usually the finest fakers when you examine an egomaniac from the start. Most interactions between egotists begin with generosity and a friendly display. They'll show you affection and praise. They will approach you with kindness and take all necessary steps to ensure that you submit to them.

You could have been quite positive that you had finally found the right person to spend the rest of your life with when you first started dating an egotist. You don't want it to stop because it seems too good for you to even consider embracing. It's possible that you were lavished with compliments, gratitude, presents, approval, outings, and meals that led you to believe that your spouse is your true love and life companion.

The admiration besieging stage is the name given to the first phase. The egotists will do all in their power at this point to convince you that they truly adore you. If you agree to this, they will be happy to trap you, replace the previous act of kindness with any form of abuse, dehumanize, and devalue you. By doing this, individuals avoid admitting they are mistaken or accepting responsibility for their actions. In light of the fact that you don't reflect their absurd ideas of who you should be or what your identity is, they will blame you for everything that occurs. Soon, as you struggle every day, all you can do is think back on the good days.

Egomaniacs, however, often give you the impression that they love you by rewarding you with vacations or presents, but this is untrue. Before you can really embrace the outward expression of rebuilt love, you are thrust back into your severe conflict and subject to yet another round of debasement. After this, you start to feel worthless, and you find yourself back where you were.

Their belief in conditional connections and enjoyment of uncertain bliss directly lead to their reason for doing this. In general, they are seeking their contentment and happiness as well as the need for them to boost their self-confidence. Egomaniacs understand that relationships are games, and that the primary focus should be on winning. They just have one concern—dominating the game. However, once they get the chance to trap you, they start to reveal their true colors by becoming cunning.

They Are Deceitful

A lot of egomaniacs might convince someone to start a relationship with them due to their engaging and vivacious personalities. Because they possess the capability to appreciate others more deeply, they are also capable of experiencing, understanding, and expressing sentiments. With this, they are also cunning and succeed in gaining people's respect and affection.

They are cunning manipulators who would do whatever to make you uneasy by disparaging you and making you feel less than.

They do this action because they are aware of your fragility and insecurity. They have confidence in bragging about deserved respect and seeking fulfillment. They are also sociable and may leave a great impression the first time you connect with them. Because of their ability to convey affection, emotion, honeyed words, and persistent assurances of submission, certain egomaniacs have all the makings of magnificent darlings. They also exaggerate in order to convince their accomplice of the intense affection they have for themselves and how they display it materially.

Egomaniacs lose interest in intimacy as soon as they're ready to locate a partner and often find it difficult to maintain a relationship for a long period or longer. They often prioritize strength above intimacy, detest vulnerability, and see this as a flaw. Since they believe they are superior to orders, they like ruling others. In this sense, they want to avoid proximity. Playing with many partners is thus the best approach to solve their problems.

The long-term effects of being in a relationship with an egotist might lead to a stunning breakup. The unexpected termination of the friendship will cause the separation to be sudden, and the ex will feel overwhelmed and confused as a result. They experience betrayal, exploitation, being used up, being crushed, and confusion. However, if they continue the relationship, they would have discovered or noticed their partner's selfishness.

Sometimes an egotist may be methodical in his approach, so he is seeing someone to focus only on his goals. He could, however, feel positively about a friend or someone who shares an interest. He misses the target on motivation to maintain a healthy connection in marriage since he wouldn't have the choice to continue being aware of the facade. When this happens, he looks for other ways to avoid becoming close by being angry, frigid, and critical.

This makes it difficult to disagree with him since doing so will result in problems. Even though egotists may sometimes satisfy the needs of their partners, they often devalue their partners and look for other opportunities to elevate their broadly enlarged inner selves. However, egotists often want to continue seeing someone and seldom ever get go of a partner as long as they continue to be important to them.

What Makes Narcissists Want to Stay?

Because of their tendency to be self-absorbed, narcissists like to stay. They must constantly convey a message to all they encounter, and having you around will improve their status and make their life more enjoyable. Egomaniacs don't care about other people's happiness or your delight, either. Because of this, it will be difficult for them to establish a fulfilling and loving relationship. They will often look at someone else, but they never seem to be really pleased.

An egotist will always look for someone to degrade in order to maintain his self-image. Therefore, he enjoys blaming others for every conflict and fight.

Even when they are mistaken, they still strive to be sorry or repent. You will be the center of attention, and you will lose the debate.

You could be wondering why they want to continue to abuse you despite all they say and how much disdain they portray for you. Following are a few explanations for why an egotist might choose to stay rather than leave, all things considered.

They wouldn't Want to Lose You as Their Assistant

Who could provide a hand around the house? Who could clean up the mess, acquire some food, and manage how the house is run? Egomaniacs tend to stay and take advantage of all of these benefits and more. That is, they are only with you because of the benefits that come with it.

They Take Great Joy in Making You Feel Unworthy.

Companions that have narcissistic tendencies like to stay since they seem to enjoy watching you suffer. They conceal this from their friends and colleagues, and some even find it difficult to believe it when they do discover it. Only a small percentage of egomaniacs are adept at concealing such tendencies.

A narcissist views losing you as failure.

An egotist wouldn't have to leave you to comprehend that they were a letdown; they could live without it. They would thus want to be with you and inflict all of the wrongdoings on you. Additionally, they often want you to fade and support their argument that you are worthless and useless.

They appreciate your reliance on them.

Your dependence on them for everything appeals to egotists. They achieved this by first showing you grace, love, and affection then vanishing once they had your attention. They develop a sour disposition and distance themselves from everything that interests you. This forces you to depend on them since their conduct has the opposite effect on your own.

An egomaniac will always come back, even if you decide to go. Although they say they're doing this to let you know they've changed, what they're really doing is giving themselves more power to dominate you the way they always did. They acknowledge their awesomeness and refuse to submit to rejection. Egomaniacs understand that they should not be despised but rather desired, and they will stop at nothing to bring you back together. If you first give an egomaniac a pass, they will continually look forward to dominating and manipulating you.

www.ingramcontent.com/pod-product-compliance
Lightning Source LLC
Chambersburg PA
CBHW050233120526
44590CB00016B/2068